Antarctica

Antarctica

BY WIL MARA

Enchantment of the World™
Second Series

CHILDREN'S PRESS®

An Imprint of Scholastic Inc.

Frontispiece: **Adélie penguin**

Consultant: Andrew Klein, PhD, Professor, Department of Geography, Texas A&M University, College Station, Texas
Please note: All statistics are as up-to-date as possible at the time of publication.

Book production by The Design Lab

Library of Congress Cataloging-in-Publication Data
Names: Mara, Wil, author.
Title: Antarctica / by Wil Mara.
Description: New York, NY : Children's Press, an imprint of Scholastic Inc.,
    2017. | Series: Enchantment of the world | Includes bibliographical
    references and index.
Identifiers: LCCN 2016025116 | ISBN 9780531220825 (library binding)
Subjects: LCSH: Antarctica—Juvenile literature.
Classification: LCC G863 .M36 2017 | DDC 919.89—dc23
LC record available at https://lccn.loc.gov/2016025116

1 2 3 4 5 6 7 8 9 10 R 26 25 24 23 22 21 20 19 18 17

Tourists viewing an iceberg

Contents

Left to right: **Ceremonial South Pole, emperor penguins, Antarctic hair grass, mossy hillside, Antarctic clothing**

CHAPTER 1

The Bottom of the World

JAYLEN IS SITTING ON THE BED IN HER DORM ROOM, exhausted after a long day's work but unable to fall asleep. She's a professor of geology on a year-long research project. She's been working on the project for just over five months. The shade on the window has been pulled all the way down, but the sun still manages to draw a bright line around it. What's strange about this—and still difficult for her to fathom—is that it's almost midnight. It's mid-January, which means the sun shines all the time. She knew Antarctica had six months of continual sunlight followed by six months of darkness, but she didn't realize how bizarre it would be until she got here. Back in her home state of Michigan, January meant winter and July meant summer. But here at the bottom of the world it's just the opposite—the warmest months are November to February, and the coldest are July to September.

Opposite: **A scientist explores an ice cave in Antarctica.**

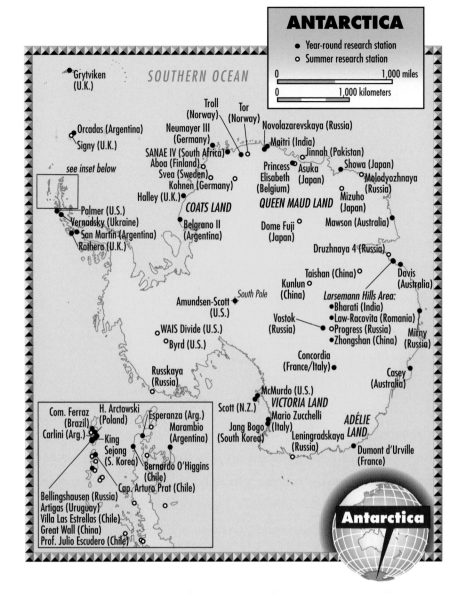

Her roommate, a biologist named Carrie, stirs in the overhead bunk. Jaylen is careful to stay as quiet as possible, for she's learned that Carrie is a light sleeper. In addition to her dorm mate, there are only about seventy other people on the whole base. It's like one giant family—and since they're basically in the middle of nowhere and depend on one another for many things, it's a giant family that needs to get along.

Jaylen thinks about her parents and her younger brother, who still lives at home. She hasn't seen them since she left and misses them very much. She talks to them on the phone, and they e-mail her a lot. But it's not the same as being there in person. She knew that would make this trip difficult, but she didn't realize just how much. She's made some friends at the station, but people come and go all the time because their projects end or they rotate out.

The easiest way for scientists to travel around Antarctica is by airplane.

She manages a tiny smile when she thinks about this coming Friday. The base is holding a party in the dining hall. There's one every month, and they're a lot of fun. Each has some silly theme—this time it's Big Band Night—and everyone does their best to dress accordingly. The party will have music and dancing and lots of food and drinks. Alec, the chef for the whole base, promised to make chocolate cream pie, Jaylen's favorite dessert. She continues to be surprised by how many different meals Alec manages to dream up—and how good they all are.

People at McMurdo Station enjoy themselves during the annual "Icestock" concert, held every year on New Year's Day.

She takes out her tablet and begins reading a novel she started last week. It's set in the Hawaiian Islands, a place she hopes to visit someday. For now, the descriptions of the warm beaches and gentle breezes in the story will have to do. It helps her escape this frigid world for a little while. She is still fascinated by Antarctica and has no regrets about working here, but she wouldn't want to live here all the time. She has discovered that she and her roommate, along with almost everyone else on the base, are in complete agreement on this.

Living in Antarctica is always a challenge. Here, a person sets up a tent in the blowing snow.

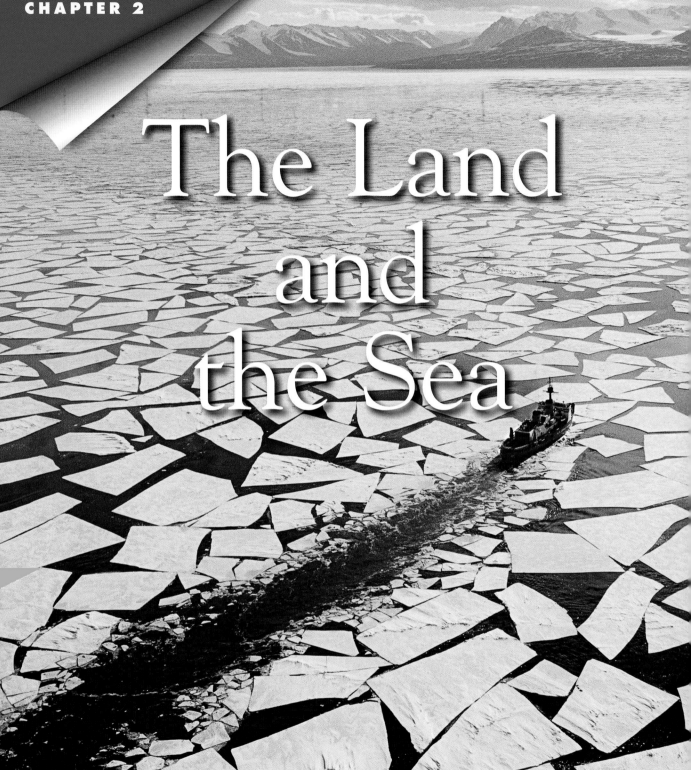

CHAPTER 2

The Land and the Sea

THE CONTINENT OF ANTARCTICA IS THE SOUTHERNMOST region on the planet, located in the heart of Earth's Southern Hemisphere. It shares this hemisphere with four other continents—all of Australia, the majority of South America, and portions of both Africa and Asia. The nation closest to Antarctica is Argentina, with Argentina's southernmost city, Ushuaia, lying roughly 770 miles (1,240 kilometers) to the north of Antarctica's northernmost area, the tip of the Antarctic Peninsula.

Opposite: **An icebreaker ship plows through ice drifting through the water near McMurdo Sound. Icebreakers create safe routes for other boats.**

The Antarctic Circle

Almost all of Antarctica lies within an imaginary circle at about 66.5°S latitude known as the Antarctic Circle. This circle represents the latitude south of which the sun is above the horizon for at least twenty-four hours in a row once a year, and below the horizon for at least twenty-four hours in a row once a year. So at the Antarctic Circle, the sun never sets on one day, about December 21, and the sun never rises on one day, about June 21.

Why the Long Days?

Continuous periods of daylight and darkness get longer nearer the poles because Earth is tilted in relation to the Sun. Earth is spinning on an axis that runs through the North and South Poles. When the part of Earth where you live is facing the Sun, it is day; when it is facing away from the Sun it is night.

Earth is also orbiting the Sun. When the part of Earth where you live is tilted toward the Sun it is summer and when it is titled away from the Sun it is winter. But the tilt of Earth is so extreme that during the summer at the South Pole, even as Earth spins, the pole is constantly lit by the Sun. And during the winter, the pole never escapes darkness.

The closer one gets to the South Pole, the southernmost point on the globe, the longer the periods of continuous daytime and continuous nighttime. The South Pole itself experiences roughly six months of continuous daylight, from mid-September to mid-March. The other six months experience continuous darkness or twilight. During the continuous daylight, the sun never moves directly overhead. Rather, it hovers just above the horizon, moving around the horizon in a counterclockwise direction all day. At the northern part of the globe, the Arctic Circle represents the same concept, except its periods of darkness and light are at opposite times of the year from when they occur in Antarctica.

A Very Big Place

Antarctica is a big place, with an area of about
miles (14,000,000 square kilometers), abou
United States and Mexico combined. It is the
seven continents, with only Europe and Austr
Antarctica is roughly circular in shape, but
tail section that flares out toward South Ame
Antarctic Peninsula. The continent has ab
(18,000 km) of coastline. Roughly 95 percer
covered by ice, while the rest is covered by r

*Main Idea –
Antarctica is
a big place.*

An Actual Pole?

Many people have wondered if there's an actual
pole at the South Pole. The answer, incredibly, is
yes. If you were to travel to the South Pole, you'd
find an outpost called the Amundsen-Scott South
Pole Station. Nearby is the Ceremonial South
Pole, which includes twelve different national
flags stuck into the icy ground in a half-circle. And
within that half-circle is another pole, just a few
feet tall, candy-striped like something in front of
a barbershop, and with a chrome sphere on top.
This is the symbolic "South Pole" that represents
Earth's southernmost location. In truth, however,
this pole is about 590 feet (180 meters) from
the actual southernmost spot on the planet, the
geographic South Pole. The coordinates of the
South Pole are simply 90°S. There is just latitude,
no longitude—because there isn't any.

The moon rises above a mountain on the Antarctic Peninsula. In Antarctica, the reflected light from the moon is surprisingly bright, allowing people to see well even when there is no sunlight.

Antarctica is the highest continent in the world. It has an average elevation of about 7,200 feet (2,200 m). Much of this elevation is a thick layer of ice. Without the ice, the continent's average elevation would probably be only about 1,500 feet (460 m).

East and West

Antarctica is generally divided into two sections—East and West Antarctica. The dividing line is the Transantarctic Mountains. This mountain chain runs across the continent from Coats Land near the Weddell Sea to Victoria Land near the Ross Sea. The Transantarctic is one of the longest mountain ranges in the world, extending about 2,175 miles (3,500 km). Its highest peak is Mount Kirkpatrick, which rises to 14,856 feet (4,528 m) above sea level.

East Antarctica (also known as Greater Antarctica) lies almost entirely within the globe's Eastern Hemisphere. It constitutes two-thirds of Antarctica's total area. The South Pole is located in this half of the continent, near the Transantarctic Mountains.

Even though East Antarctica is almost entirely covered by ice, its coastal regions support life. Various animals live and breed along the coast all year long, including penguins, petrels, and seals. Antarctica is protected by internationally recognized laws that forbid human interference, including

The peaks of the Transantarctic Mountains are little more than barren rock.

hunting, industrial activity, and weapons testing. As a result, there has been little human interaction with the area, making it one of the few unexplored places left on earth.

West Antarctica is the smaller of the pair (thus it is sometimes called Lesser Antarctica), and the bulk of it lies within Earth's Western Hemisphere. It constitutes just one-third of the continent's total area. The main feature of West Antarctica is the Antarctic Peninsula, which is the only part of Antarctica that warms up in the summer to the point where the ice will melt away to expose the ground beneath. During this period mosses and some grasses flourish, enjoying a brief growth cycle. The ice sheet in West Antarctica is much thinner than it is in East Antarctica. The base of the ice sheet is also below sea level. This means that if all the ice in

Moss grows along the coast of the Antarctic Peninsula.

Antarctica melted, the Antarctic Peninsula would be a string of islands rather than a solid stretch of land.

West Antarctica also features active volcanoes. Mount Erebus, the world's southernmost active volcano, lies on Ross Island, just off the mainland in the Ross Sea. It reaches an elevation of 12,448 feet (3,794 m). Atop the mountain is a crater containing a lake of lava, which frequently explodes with lava bombs, molten rocks that harden when they land. Elsewhere on Mount Erebus are towers of ice that form around vents where gas and steam are escaping from beneath the ground.

Even taller than Erebus is Mount Sidley, which soars to 14,058 feet (4,285 m). It is the highest dormant volcano in Antarctica.

The highest point in West Antarctica—and, in fact, the entire continent—is Mount Vinson. This mountain, which lies at the base of the Antarctic Peninsula, rises 16,050 feet (4,892 m) above sea level.

Antarctica's Geographic Features

Area: 5,400,000 square miles (14,000,000 sq km)

Southernmost Point: South Pole, 90°S latitude and 0° longitude

Northernmost Point: Prime Head, at the northern tip of the Antarctic Peninsula

Highest Elevation: Mount Vinson, 16,050 feet (4,892 m) above sea level

Lowest Elevation: Bentley Subglacial Trench, 8,383 feet (2,555 m) below sea level

Average Annual Precipitation: 6.5 inches (17 cm)

Average High Temperature: At McMurdo Station, 32°F (0°C) in January, –7°F (–22°C) in July; at the South Pole, –15°F (–26°C) in January, –69°F (–56°C) in July

Average Low Temperature: At McMurdo Station, 22°F (–5.5°C) in January, –22°F (–30°C) in July; at the South Pole, –21°F (–29°C) in January, –81°F (–63°C) in July

Coldest Recorded Temperature: –136°F (–93°C) in August 2010

Warmest Recorded Temperature: 63.5°F (17.5°C) on March 24, 2015, at Hope Bay, on the Trinity Peninsula

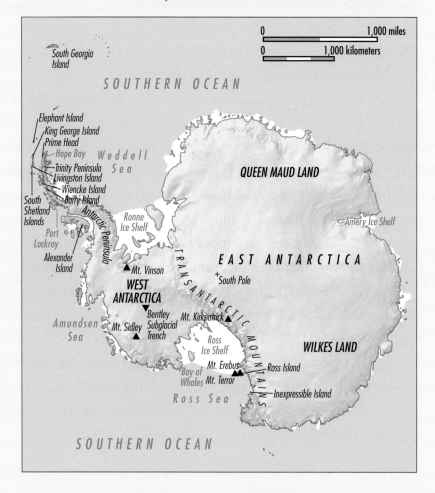

Islands

Antarctica includes hundreds of islands. Most are similar to the main continent in that they feature rock, ice, snow, high winds, and freezing temperatures. The largest is Alexander Island, which lies off the west coast of the Antarctic Peninsula.

Humans have not set foot on most of Antarctica's islands. There are notable exceptions, however. A few are home to scientific research stations. Some have become tourist destinations. For example, the South Shetland Islands, a small island group located about 75 miles (120 km) off the end of the Antarctic Peninsula, have been a tourist destination since the 1950s.

Snow and Ice

When you think of a desert, you probably imagine a great expanse of sand in all directions, baking under the brutal heat of an unforgiving sun. But if you consider the definition of the word—that it gets almost no precipitation—then you'll understand why Antarctica is also characterized as a desert. On average, it receives about 6 to 8 inches (15 to 20 centimeters) of precipitation over an entire year;

Deep cracks in the ice called crevasses make traveling in Antarctica hazardous.

and during some years, parts of the continent do not receive even 1 inch (2.5 cm) of precipitation. Most of the precipitation—which almost always comes in the form of snow rather than rain—occurs along the northern coastal areas, leaving the inland regions among the driest places in the world.

Roughly 95 percent of Antarctica is covered in ice—and not just a few inches of it, but ice with an average depth of more than a mile (1.6 km). This ice mass is known as the Antarctic Ice Sheet and is the largest of its kind in the world. About 90 percent of the naturally occurring ice on the planet—along with roughly 60 percent of all the world's fresh water—is found in the Antarctic Ice Sheet.

Melting Ice

The average temperature around the globe is increasing. Much of this is caused by human activity. For example, burning oil to power cars sends pollutants into the air. Some of these, such as carbon dioxide, trap heat near the earth rather than letting it pass through the atmosphere and out into space.

The warming of Earth is causing glaciers to weaken and melt around the world. In Antarctica, the West Antarctic Ice Sheet is shrinking. As the water that had been bound up in ice becomes liquid again, sea levels rise. Experts estimate that by the year 2100, the sea level will be 1 to 6 feet (30 cm to 2 m) higher than it is now. This could devastate cities, communities, and environments around the globe. In Antarctica itself, this could destroy many colonies of Adélie penguins, causing their population to drop by half.

Cold and Colder

There's no place colder than Antarctica, and its temperature statistics are astonishing. In the Antarctic winter—which runs from March through September when the Northern Hemisphere is enjoying spring and summer—the temperature can drop to the –80s Fahrenheit (–60s Celsius). In the Antarctic summer—October through February—the continent warms up to an average of about –15°F (–26°C), and temperatures go even higher along the northern coasts, which can exceed zero and sometimes reach above 50°F (10°C) during the height of summer.

These temperatures feel even colder in the continent's nearly constant winds. Winds are strongest along the coastline. Farther inland, they are usually not so powerful but still blow frequently. Because the strong winds pick up blowing snow, the winds often cause whiteouts.

Penguins in a snowstorm on an island near the Antarctic Peninsula. More snow falls in the peninsula than in any other part of Antarctica.

An iceberg floats in the ocean near East Antarctica.

The Surrounding Ocean

Antarctica is surrounded by a body of water commonly known as the Southern Ocean. The Southern Ocean is found south of the 60°S line of latitude. Like Antarctica itself, the Southern Ocean is frigid. Parts of it freeze in the winter months, forming sea ice. Ice also breaks off Antarctica's glaciers and ice shelves along the coast, a process called calving. The ice that has broken off forms icebergs that float in the water, even during the summer. High winds on the ocean not only drive temperatures lower but also help build large, powerful waves. Some of the southerly parts of the Southern Ocean experience the most powerful continuous winds in the world.

A number of regions of the Southern Ocean are known as seas. These are regions that are surrounded, in part, by land. Among the most significant is the Amundsen Sea, which lies off the continent's southwestern coast. While the Amundsen is almost entirely covered with ice, scientists believe it is the site of ongoing volcanic activity, which has altered both local water temperatures and the movement of icebergs and glaciers. The Ross Sea, south of New Zealand, is one of the least icy of the areas surrounding Antarctica. The Weddell Sea lies southeast of South America. High winds and ice-riddled waters have made sailing through the Weddell Sea very risky, causing some notable tragedies in years past. Early explorers have remarked upon the contrast between the Weddell's harsh environment and the Ross's more accommodating clime.

Meet Mr. Ross

Antarctica's Ross Sea is named after James Clark Ross, a British explorer who discovered it in 1841. Ross seemed to like polar extremes—he went to the Arctic in 1818 along with his uncle Sir John Ross, and in the following nine years he visited the Arctic four more times with Sir William Parry, another British explorer. Then, in 1829, he joined John Ross for another Arctic journey. On this expedition, he and his uncle became the first people to discover the location of the magnetic North Pole. Ross left Great Britain in 1841 and headed south for a change, eventually entering the Southern Ocean and discovering the sea that would one day bear his name. This expedition also discovered two volcanoes, which were named for the expedition's two ships, the *Erebus* and the *Terror*. Today, the Ross Sea is renowned for being rich in biodiversity, or the variety of species that live there. It is home to a variety of penguins, seals, whales, fish, and smaller creatures.

CHAPTER 3

Living Things

THE CONTINENT OF ANTARCTICA LACKS THE DIVERSITY of life found in other parts of the world. Yet many living things not only survive in this frigid frontier but thrive there.

Antarctica has a much simpler food web than most places. Many creatures in the Antarctic, both large and small, depend on krill as a major source of food. Krill are tiny sea creatures that are eaten by birds and fish, seals and whales. Though the animals supplement their diet with other food, the krill are vital to their survival.

Mammals

The mammals native to Antarctica rely on the ocean for their survival. They include seals, whales, and porpoises.

Antarctica is home to several seal species. They all have long, sleek, blubbery bodies; large, mournful eyes; and front limbs that act as flippers in the water and feet on land. Their sight and hearing are excellent both in and out of the water, helping them avoid the many animals that consider them prey.

Opposite: **Elephant seal pups relax on South Georgia Island. Adult elephant seals are the world's largest land carnivores, weighing more than six times as much as polar bears.**

The whale is
1 of Antartica's
inspiring
animals.

A humbback whale breaches, or leaps, from the water, near the Antarctic coast. Scientists are not sure why whales breach. Perhaps it is to communicate with other whales or to knock parasites from their skin, or perhaps it is just fun.

...ecies include the crabeater ... seal, and the leopard seal. ... most abundant species on ... ner months, when 95 per-...imals—gather near South Georgia Island, which lies northeast of the Antarctic Peninsula.

One of the most awe-inspiring of Antarctica's residents is the whale. About twenty whale species are found in the Antarctic region. The most common include the humpback, the minke, and the orca. Some whales are extremely large. The blue whale is the largest creature ever to live on earth. It can grow to 100 feet (30 m) in length and weigh in excess of 200 tons. It is long and graceful, with a blue-gray cast that is dark above and a bit lighter underneath.

Whales evolved from land-dwelling mammals (their closest current relative is the hippopotamus), but they live their entire lives in the water. They eat, breed, and raise their young in the water. Nevertheless, they do not breathe through gills like fish, but instead come to the surface from time to time to refill their lungs. Their blowholes are, in fact, similar in structure to human nostrils. Whales are warm-blooded, and the heavy layers of blubber (fat) beneath their skin enable them to maintain a high level of internal warmth within Antarctica's frigid waters. All whales are carnivores, meaning they eat animals. The primary food for many whales are tiny krill. Adult blue whales consume about 4 tons of food, mainly krill, each day. Other whales eat fish, squid, and crabs. Some orcas even eat larger animals such as seals.

Krill are related to shrimp. They range in size from about 0.25 to 2 inches (0.5 to 5 cm) long.

Birds

Dozens of kinds of birds live in Antarctica. These include petrels, cormorants, sheathbills, and several species of penguins, including the emperor penguin and the Adélie penguin. Most Antarctic birds get their food from the sea. Petrels scoop up krill and fish from the surface while cormorants sometimes dive deep for their dinner.

Penguins are probably the best known of the Antarctic bird species. Penguins cannot fly in the air. Their wings have evolved instead into functional flippers, which allow them to "fly" through the water. This is particularly useful to them as

A giant petrel swoops down over the South Shetland Islands. Petrels snatch fish and krill from the water, but they are also scavengers, feeding on the bodies of penguins, seals, and other animals that have died.

All Hail the Emperor

The largest penguin found in Antarctica—and anywhere else in the world—is the emperor penguin. Average adults reach about 4 feet (1.2 m) tall and weigh between 60 and 100 pounds (27 and 45 kilograms). The emperor penguin is endemic to Antarctica, meaning it is found nowhere else on earth. They breed during the chilly Antarctic winters, where some penguins travel as far as 65 miles (105 km) to gather in huge colonies. A female emperor penguin lays just a single egg. She then passes it to the male, who protects the egg by balancing it on its feet and sheltering it with its skin to keep it warm. Once the chick hatches, both parents care for the young penguin until it is able to venture into the Antarctic wilderness on its own.

they spend about half of their lives in the water. And don't misinterpret their round, waddling bodies as evidence of awkwardness—they are superb swimmers. Penguins are meat eaters, subsisting on a diet of krill, fish, some crabs, squid, and a variety of other sea life. Some can dive far below the surface of the water, sometimes going down 150 feet (45 m) to find food. Like some other Antarctic creatures, they have a layer of blubber that allows them to endure their cold surroundings.

Sea Life

The Antarctic waters are home to many sea creatures. These range from tiny krill to huge squid. Squid are like something out of science fiction. They have long, tubular bodies with wavy tentacles at one end and round, gazing eyeballs set somewhere

Mysterious Creature

One species of squid commands a great deal of attention in the Antarctic waters. The colossal squid lives up to its name, with the average adult measuring about 35 feet (11 m) long and weighing around 1,500 pounds (680 kg). Despite their huge size, very few colossal squid have ever been found, so knowledge of them is scant. They are believed to feed mainly on a large species of fish called toothfish, hunting them possibly by lying motionless until unsuspecting prey happens by. The colossal squid itself forms part of the diet of the sperm whale and other whale species.

in the middle. The squid's body, called its mantle, includes a pair of fins to help it steer, and gills, which it uses to breathe. The squid also has a siphon, like a short hose, that it uses to propel itself. The squid's long tentacles can grab and hold things with a system of hooks and suckers. Squid are found in most ocean waters around the globe and there are hundreds of different species. The Southern Ocean is home to species such as the warty squid, the giant squid, and the colossal squid.

Other sea creatures in Antarctica are crabs, clams, and sea urchins. Fish that thrive in the cold Antarctic waters include some species of cod, mackerel, lantern fish, skates, and toothfish. To survive in the most frigid waters, the fish must have unusual adaptations. The Antarctic toothfish, for example, has antifreeze proteins in its blood.

Plant Life

Antarctica might be the last place you'd expect to see grass. But in the right part of the continent, at the right time of the year, grass grows there. The Antarctic is home to two native grass species—Antarctic hair grass and Antarctic pearlwort. In summer, in the more northerly parts of the continent, the ice and snow melt just enough and the temperatures rise just enough for these species to grow.

One of the keys to the survival of these grasses is their ability to absorb nitrogen much faster than similar grass species in warmer climates. In fact, they absorb nitrogen up to 150 times as fast. They draw nitrogen from rotting plant matter and animal

Antarctic hair grass grows quickly in December, January, and February before going dormant again as the weather gets colder.

waste that stay frozen for most of the year. Once that matter begins to defrost in the summer, the grasses can absorb the nitrogen and grow quickly. The effects of global warming have been particularly dramatic in Earth's polar regions. This has lengthened the period of time that organic matter can defrost and decompose, enabling the grasses to thrive like never before.

A third species of grass, annual bluegrass, is now growing in Antarctica but is not native to the region. It was introduced on a few islands beyond the peninsula. It is an invasive species, spreading easily, especially with the warmer weather, and forcing out the native grasses.

In the Antarctic regions where annual bluegrass has spread, the amount of Antarctic hair grass and Antarctic pearlwort has declined.

A variety of mosses survive in some parts of the frigid Antarctic landscape. A moss is a tiny plant that does not flower and usually occurs in thick mats, favoring damp locations that receive little light. Most moss species grow only an inch or two (2.5 to 5 cm) in height and have a greenish, velvety appearance. While modest in appearance, moss can be quite tough and hardy, enabling it to survive in Antarctica. But as with other Antarctic plants, mosses occur only in the area of the Antarctic Peninsula, both along the coast and on a handful of islands. Elephant Island, for example, is the site of a 5,500-year-old moss bank that is one of the oldest living things on earth.

A mossy hillside on the Antarctic Peninsula. More than one hundred different species of moss grow in Antarctica.

Living Things **37**

How Does It Survive?

The secrets to a moss's ability to thrive in Antarctica are varied. For one, it stays close to the ground, avoiding the devastating effects of the freezing winds. The continent's long periods of darkness are ideal for moss, as is the relatively low intensity of light when the sun does shine. Antarctic moss has also developed a tremendous tolerance for the cold, able to essentially shut down during the most frigid times of the year and then return to an active state when the temperatures begin rising again.

Liverworts are similar to mosses in many respects. They are hardy enough to grow in a variety of climates, are generally very small, and can cover broad areas in a kind of thick carpet that is usually green. Some species produce leaves and flowers.

The Antarctic region is home to roughly two dozen liverwort species. As with the mosses, they are found in the more northerly regions of the continent and thrive only in the summer months. They cling to the rocky surface, preferring areas with minimal sunlight and some moisture. Antarctic liverworts grow in tighter groups than liverworts in warmer climates, so they retain as much moisture as possible.

Fungi and Algae

Many forms of fungi live in Antarctica—more than a thousand types have been discovered so far. Fungi are living organisms but are not plants and not animals. Mold is a form of fungus. So are mushrooms and yeast. Fungi are a kind of parasite, attaching themselves to living plants for survival. Fungi are hardy and highly adaptable, and scientists believe there are millions of species found in every environment around the world. In the colder areas of the Antarctic, ground fungus can be difficult to detect without proper equipment, because it is embedded deep in the soil. In warmer Antarctic regions, some fungi produce mushrooms at warmer times of year.

There is no set definition of algae, nor can scientists even agree on whether or not algae are plants or, like fungi, their own, unique category. Seaweed is a form of algae. Some forms

Lichen is an organism in which fungi and algae or bacteria work together. Lichens often grow on exposed rock in Antarctica.

Algae covers a glacier in Antarctica.

of algae can flourish in Antarctica's bitter conditions. Species have been found in the soil, on rocks, in the snow, in the ice, and in all liquid water throughout the region. In the warmer months, snow-dwelling species become so widespread that they can tint the snow various colors (green, orange, and red are common). About seven hundred forms of algae are known to exist in Antarctica. One of the most important is the ocean-dwelling phytoplankton. Like plants, they convert light energy from the sun and carbon dioxide into sugar. Phytoplankton are the base of the ocean's food web.

Conservation

One of the earliest efforts at protecting Antarctica came in 1959, with the signing of the Antarctic Treaty System. The treaty stated that the Antarctic area was to be used only for peaceful purposes such as education, and banned activities such as military exercises, weapons testing, and armed conflict. The treaty also forbade dumping of harmful waste material in the region. Twelve countries signed the Antarctic Treaty System in 1959, and by 2016, fifty-three countries had agreed to it.

Countries have also made their own laws and regulations related to Antarctica. In 1978, the United States Congress passed the Antarctic Conservation Act. This law barred American citizens from collecting any native Antarctic animal or plant species, from transporting Antarctic species into the United States, and from introducing any foreign species into Antarctica. The act also made it illegal for companies to discharge toxic matter or other pollutants into the region.

Protecting Antarctica

Today, many different groups are involved in protecting Antarctica. These include the Antarctic and Southern Ocean Coalition, the Antarctic Ocean Alliance, and the Antarctican Society. These groups have worked with governmental agencies to further conservation efforts. They have educated the public on the status of Antarctic conservation and how they can help; helped manage the region's ecological treasures; supported researchers in the area; assured that international laws are being honored; and reported instances of criminal activity. Another group, the International Association of Antarctica Tour Operators, works to promote environmentally responsible travel.

CHAPTER 4

Heroic History

ANTARCTICA HAS AN UNUSUAL HISTORY. HUMANS
have populated it for only about a hundred years—a mere
instant on the grand scale of time. And yet people have managed to accomplish quite a bit in that brief period.

Opposite: **Ships sail in the icy waters near Antarctica.**

Land to the South

More than two thousand years ago, mapmakers and explorers
theorized that there was likely a giant landmass to be found
at the "bottom" of Earth. Part of this logic was born from the
belief that the Southern Hemisphere had to have roughly the
same amount of land as the Northern Hemisphere.

Explorers began attempting to solve this mystery in the
mid-1400s, daring to sail farther south than ever before. In
1473, Portugal native Lopes Gonçalves led the first European
sea journey across the equator into the Southern Hemisphere.
Bartolomeu Dias, another Portuguese adventurer, took a crew
around the southern tip of Africa in 1487 while searching for

In 1519, Ferdinand Magellan left Spain with five ships and about 270 men to find a westward route to Asia. He died in the Philippines, but one of his ships returned to Spain in 1522, completing the first journey around the globe.

trade routes to India. The mere fact that they found the southern tip of Africa suggested that there might be more land even farther south. A third Portuguese man, Ferdinand Magellan, led a Spanish expedition around South America in the early

Mapping Unknown Lands

By the late 1500s, mapmakers were including a broad landmass along the southern edge of the world even though no one had actually been there yet. Perhaps to underscore their uncertainty, this region was sometimes called Terra Australis Nondum Cognita, which means "southern land not yet known" in Latin. Gerardus Mercator, a Flemish cartographer, or mapmaker, from what is now Belgium, came to believe in the existence of Terra Australis. Another Flemish mapmaker, Cornelius Wytfliet, went a step farther in 1597 when he wrote, "The terra Australis is therefore the southernmost of all other lands."

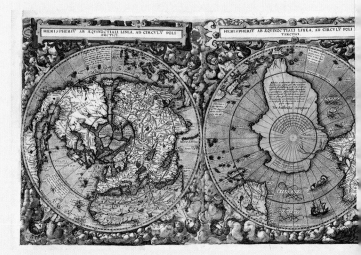

1500s and came across the islands of Tierra del Fuego, the southernmost part of that continent. He also suspected there was more land to be found farther south.

The Search Is On

Stirred into a near frenzy by so much theorizing and so little hard evidence, many explorers decided to undertake the challenge to become the first to set foot on the southern land.

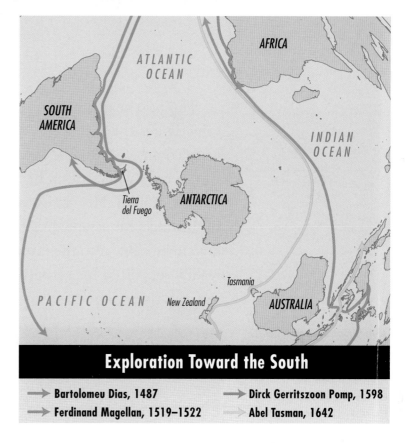

Exploration Toward the South

→ Bartolomeu Dias, 1487
→ Ferdinand Magellan, 1519–1522
→ Dirck Gerritszoon Pomp, 1598
→ Abel Tasman, 1642

In 1642, a Dutch sailor named Abel Tasman headed south of Australia to see what he could find. During the journey, Tasman and his crew made some remarkable discoveries. One was the fact that Australia had a southern coast and there-fore—contrary to the belief held by some—did not stretch all the way to the South Pole. He reached the same conclusion that Magellan did when he found Tierra del Fuego—that if there was more sea to the south, then there just might be more land as well. Tasman also became the first European to discover the lands now known as New Zealand and Tasmania. Because of the chilly weather he encountered during the southernmost parts of the journey, Tasman came to wonder if New Zealand were actually part of the fabled Terra Australis continent.

The next major step in the search for the southern lands came under the leadership of explorer James Cook. A man who led an adventurous and seafaring life, Cook was in the British navy while still in his teens and eventually rose to the rank of captain. His navigating skills were excellent, as were his instincts for accurate cartography. Intelligent and fiercely driven, he came into the favor of many in British society, who readily supported his activities during a period when Britain was eagerly trying to expand its global influence. Cook led

James Cook began his voyages of exploration in 1768. In the decade that followed, he circled the globe twice, traveling to the Arctic and the Antarctic, around Australia, up the west coast of North America, and more.

two vessels into southern seas for a long journey beginning in 1772, and in mid-January 1773, he and his crew became the first humans to cross what is known today as the Antarctic Circle. His southward progress was halted by ice floes, however. The ice and the frigid weather forced him to return north. Undeterred, he went back the following December, crossing the Antarctic Circle again. He went a third time in early 1774. Each time, he was stopped by ice, and upon his return he reported that there was likely no land of importance or value farther south. People had thought that the land to the south would be lush and extensive. Cook concluded that if there was a southern continent, it was much smaller and colder than had been imagined.

James Cook was sailing on the *Endeavour* (above) when he neared Antarctica. The ninety-four people on the ship included sailors, soldiers, and scientists.

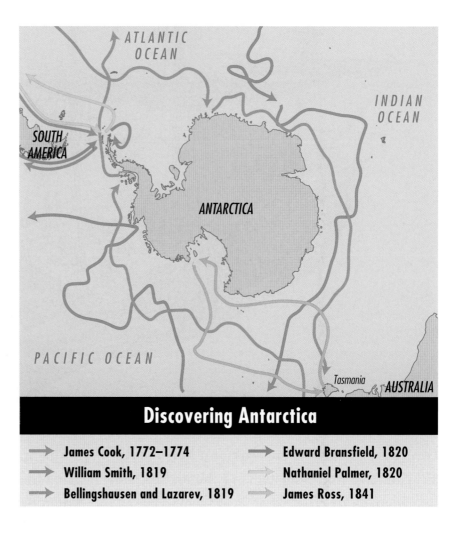

ATLANTIC OCEAN

INDIAN OCEAN

SOUTH AMERICA

ANTARCTICA

PACIFIC OCEAN

Tasmania AUSTRALIA

Discovering Antarctica

→ James Cook, 1772–1774   → Edward Bransfield, 1820
→ William Smith, 1819   → Nathaniel Palmer, 1820
→ Bellingshausen and Lazarev, 1819   → James Ross, 1841

Found!

Despite Cook's declaration, the race was still on to be the first person to find undeniable proof of the Antarctic continent's existence. Ironically, the person who finally reached this goal wasn't even trying to achieve it.

William Smith, who had been born in England in 1790, wanted to be a sailor from an early age. He began his apprenticeship while in his early teens and was co-owner of a boat by his early twenties. The boat, called the *Williams*, was meant to

Who Was First?

A Dutch sailor named Dirck Gerritszoon Pomp was in the Antarctic area more than two hundred years before William Smith. Born in Holland in 1544, Pomp grew up in Portugal and became a merchant in coastal India. During the course of his duties, he sailed to both Japan and China, possibly becoming the first Dutch person ever to do so. He developed a fascination with Asian cultures and a love of sea travel in general. Gradually, Pomp moved away from his work as a merchant and began to embrace the life of an adventurer.

During a journey in 1598, Pomp was leading his ship around the southern tip of South America. The ship was driven off course by heavy winds and forced southward toward Antarctica. When the vessel entered an area around 64°S latitude, Pomp claimed to have spotted icy, mountainous land. This sighting has never been conclusively confirmed, but if it's true, it was likely an area in the South Shetland Islands group. This would make Pomp's crew the first to see Antarctic land, a significant achievement in human exploration.

When William Smith landed on King George Island (above) in 1819, he became the first person to set foot on Antarctic lands.

be used for trade. In February 1819, while transporting a load of cargo, Smith guided his ship around Cape Horn, part of Tierra del Fuego, with the hope of catching some strong winds to help the ship along. His ship drifted too far south, however, and on February 19 he spotted what would become known as the South Shetland Islands. These islands are located along the northern tip of the Antarctic Peninsula. Specifically, it is believed he saw what is known today as Livingston Island.

Unsure of what it was, Smith simply made a note of it before getting back on course. When he reported the sighting, however, his superiors scoffed at the claim. More interested in commerce than exploration, Smith thought little more of the discovery until he was back in the area six months later. On October 16, he made a point of mooring off the coast of the largest island and venturing out to explore. His landing marks the first time a human being made physical contact with Antarctic lands.

Nathaniel Palmer

Sensing that he had crossed into unknown territory, Smith gave the island a name—King George Island, in honor of King George III, the ruler of the United Kingdom. He also named the island group as a whole, calling them the South Shetland Islands in honor of Scotland's Shetland Islands.

Nathaniel Palmer led the first group of Americans to discover Antarctica. Palmer Land, part of the Antarctic Peninsula, is named for him.

Finding the Antarctic Peninsula

In 1820, the British Royal Navy sent Smith and a team led by Edward Bransfield back to explore the area more thoroughly. On January 30, Bransfield saw the northern tip of the Antarctic Peninsula. Yet he may not have been the first to see mainland Antarctica. In 1819, Russia had sent Fabian Gottlieb von Bellingshausen and Mikhail Lazarev to lead an

Whale hunters stand on the back of a huge blue whale they caught in Antarctica. Many of the people who traveled to the Southern Ocean in the 1800s and early 1900s were whalers.

expedition to explore the Southern Ocean. They probably saw the continent just two days before Bransfield. By some accounts, however, the Russian team did not realize it was part of the main continent rather than an island. Later that same year, an American named Nathaniel Palmer also sighted the coast of Antarctica during his search for seal colonies.

A New Frontier

Once the existence of Antarctica was proved, many people became interested in exploring it. This period, sometimes called the Heroic Age of Antarctic Exploration, would last into the twentieth century. Countries from all over the globe sent sailors to gather as much knowledge as they could about this exciting new frontier. They wanted to accurately map the area, to determine if it had any economic value, and to assess its importance with regard to the earth's weather patterns and conditions. The bitter Antarctic conditions caused some expeditions to unfold very differently than planned, with a few resulting in tragedy on a grand scale. Others, however, provided scientific information that is still used today.

Whale and seal hunters, as well as several government-sponsored explorers, investigated the Antarctic coastline in the mid-1800s. But the first major effort to research the area properly was most likely the Belgian Antarctic Expedition, which took place from 1897 to 1899. The expedition's ship, called the *Belgica*, became trapped in ice floes when it got close to the Antarctic coast and remained there for the Antarctic

The crew of the *Belgica* included people from several different countries, including Belgium, Norway, Poland, and Romania.

winter. The crew became seriously ill, and a few died. Although the daylight eventually returned, it was several months more before the crew managed to free their ship from the ice. Finally, after being trapped in the ice for nearly a year, the *Belgica* sailed homeward. The ship reached the Chilean city of Punta Arenas at the end of March 1899. The men were weary from the harrowing excursion but loaded with scientific data.

To the Pole!

In 1901, the British National Antarctic Expedition, known as the Discovery Expedition, set sail under the command of

Robert F. Scott led two expeditions to Antarctica in the early 1900s.

British navy captain Robert Falcon Scott. Its goal was to gather scientific information and explore south, toward the pole. During the three-year journey, Scott and his team explored the continent, but they did not make an effort to reach the pole.

Ernest Shackleton, a member of Scott's team, led his own expedition from 1907 to 1909. Shackleton and three of his men attempted to reach the South Pole, coming within about 90 miles (145 km) of it before being forced to turn back. Disappointed but glad to be alive, Shackleton wrote to his wife, "I thought you'd rather have a live donkey than a dead lion."

However, it was neither Scott nor Shackleton but Roald Amundsen, a member of the *Belgica*'s crew, who would finally make Antarctic history. In 1910, Amundsen led a team to the area in his quest to be the first person to reach the Geographic South Pole. Amundsen made the decision to go to the South Pole suddenly and did not tell most of his crew where they were headed until they set sail. He left Norway in August on the polar exploration ship the *Fram* and landed at the Bay of Whales in the Ross Sea in January 1911. There, he and his crew set up their base, known as Framheim. The crew had to make extensive preparations

Roald Amundsen's men anchored their ship, the *Fram*, to the ice in the Bay of Whales along the Ross Ice Shelf. The ship remained there for a year while Amundsen and his team made their South Pole expedition.

Roald Amundsen used sled dogs to travel to the South Pole.

before trying to reach the pole. Most importantly, they had to create numerous depots along the route. These were stores of essential supplies such as food and oil to start and maintain fires for cooking and heating. It took months to make these preparations. By the time they had managed to establish just three depots, it was late April and the Antarctic winter was upon them. So they had to wait.

Their approach to the South Pole finally began on October 19, 1911. As luck would have it, the weather took a bitter turn soon after they set out, but Amundsen did not want to go back. He nearly lost his life when a snow bridge collapsed beneath him. Then, in mid-November, the team encountered the Transantarctic Mountains, which took nearly two weeks to pass simply because the team had trouble finding a safe route. In the weeks that followed, the men had to deal with diminishing food supplies, increasingly difficult weather conditions, and snow that covered holes in the ice into which one could easily fall and be lost forever. But they pressed on, and on December 14, became the first humans to reach the South Pole. Amundsen erected a Norwegian flag to mark the feat. After he returned to Framheim and set sail for home in late January, he sent out telegrams letting the world know of his stunning achievement.

There was one tragic end note to Amundsen's victory. Robert Falcon Scott had hopes of reaching the South Pole the same year. He and his team approached the journey from a different starting point and arrived at the pole only a brief time after Amundsen—thirty-three days to be exact. But he and his team had so exhausted their supplies as well as themselves that their return journey was all but doomed. Scott and his four companions died from the cold and a lack of food just 11 miles (18 km) from a food depot.

In the Years Since

In the years after Amundsen's triumph, other attempts at exploring Antarctica met with varying degrees of success. A German

Amundsen's Tent

At the South Pole is a flagpole that was erected in 1965 by an Argentine expedition. Not far from the pole is the actual tent that Roald Amundsen pitched in 1911. Visitors can't actually see the tent, though, because it is buried under ice and snow. Nevertheless, Amundsen's tent has been declared a historic site, and there are plans to dig it out in the future.

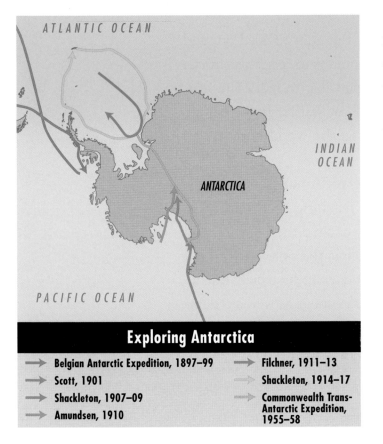

ATLANTIC OCEAN

INDIAN
OCEAN

ANTARCTICA

PACIFIC OCEAN

Exploring Antarctica

→ Belgian Antarctic Expedition, 1897–99
→ Scott, 1901
→ Shackleton, 1907–09
→ Amundsen, 1910

→ Filchner, 1911–13
→ Shackleton, 1914–17
→ Commonwealth Trans-Antarctic Expedition, 1955–58

named Wilhelm Filchner tried to cross the whole of the Antarctic mainland from 1911 to 1913, but that expedition never got started because its ship became trapped in pack ice.

Ernest Shackleton made the same attempt from 1914 to 1917. His ship became trapped in the ice in the Weddell Sea in January 1915. The following October, as the ice was breaking up, it crushed the ship. Shackleon and his crew abandoned ship and were forced to camp on the floating ice. It would be another six months before they reached remote Elephant Island, and another two-week journey in a lifeboat to reach South Georgia Island, where there was a whaling station where they could get help. Despite the incredible hardships, all of Shackleton's party survived. A second team, however, had attempted to lay out depots in support of Shackleton's group from the Ross Sea side of the continent, and three men died as a result.

It wasn't until the Commonwealth Trans-Antarctic Expedition of 1955 to 1958 that humans successfully crossed the continent. This expedition was sponsored by a half dozen countries and led by two veteran explorers, Englishman

Vivian Fuchs and New Zealander Sir Edmund Hillary. Hillary had already gained fame when he became the first person to reach the top of Mount Everest, the highest mountain in the world. The Commonwealth Trans-Antarctic Expedition took just ninety-nine days to complete the historic journey.

Today, with the great advantages of technology and existing scientific knowledge, travel throughout the Antarctic continent is not as treacherous as it was a century ago. Researchers make such treks on a regular basis, and research sites have been established in areas where humans could not have survived in the past.

Members of Ernest Shackleton's team play soccer in 1915, while their ship, the *Endurance*, is frozen in the ice.

CHAPTER 5

Communal Governance

ANTARCTICA HAS NO PERMANENT RESIDENTS, NO towns or cities, and no significant economic activity. As such, it is not surprising that it does not have its own government. It does, however, have an administrative body that looks after it today.

Early Claims of Sovereignty

Almost from the moment humans descended upon Antarctic land, world governments were making claims of sovereignty (the state of having power over something) in the Antarctic region. The British were among the first. Since the early 1800s, they had claimed authority over the Falkland Islands, which lie just southeast of South America's southernmost tip. In 1908, they extended this authority to northern parts of the Antarctic Peninsula, mainly to regulate commercial fishing in the area. Since this claim met with little international resistance, the British changed the wording of their claim less than ten years later. The result was an attempt at sovereignty over the majority of the peninsula all the way to the South Pole.

In the 1920s, Britain made some quiet efforts toward asserting control over the entire continent. Other governments then stepped in. France, Norway, Argentina, and Chile all came forward with their own claims. The French had already claimed a narrow strip south of Australia as their own, because a Frenchman, named Jules Dumont d'Urville, had arrived there first, in 1840. Norway was concerned about fishing interests. Whaling in particular was a profitable business

Jules Dumont d'Urville journeyed to Antarctica in 1840. His men mapped part of the coast, which France claimed. This area is called Adélie Land, after d'Urville's wife.

in the Southern Ocean. The Norwegians were concerned that the British would try to control the area with their own ships, denying others entry into rich whaling zones or charging whalers high taxes.

In South America, Chile had grown into a significant power. Chileans had already been using some Antarctic areas for their commercial interests, so they had no intention of allowing the British to take control. They made clear which areas these were through the establishment

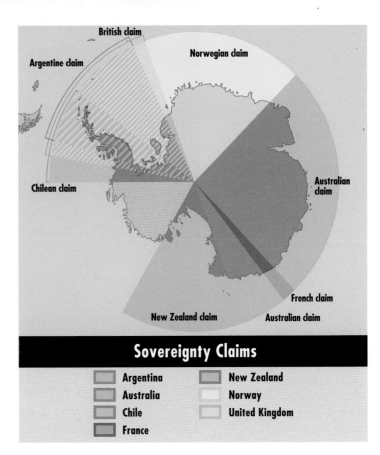

of what formally became known as the Chilean Antarctic Territory. Long before the British became involved, the Chilean government was recognized by many as having authority over certain parts of the continent. British explorer Robert Scott, for example, made a point of getting the Chilean government's permission before turning his ships south during his own expeditions. Argentina's complaints were similar to Chile's, as they already had an established presence in the area and no intentions of surrendering their authority to anyone. The British tried anyway, presuming that they had the power to grant the Argentines permission to continue their interests. But the Argentines did not accept this, and tensions continued to rise.

Chilean president Gabriel González Videla supported Chile's land claims in Antarctica. In the 1940s, he became the first head of state of any nation to visit the continent.

Trying to Get Along

The British did make some concessions to the other nations in an attempt to settle the situation. In the late 1930s, they recognized the claims made by France and Norway. France then had control over Adélie Land, named after the wife of the explorer who discovered it. And Norway received a wide slice of the region of Antarctica south of Africa—since named Queen Maud Land—as well as many islands. The claims of Chile and Argentina were recognized in 1940 and 1943, respectively. Australia and New Zealand, both former British colonies, each had their own claims. New Zealand oversaw a small slice of Antarctica called the Ross Dependency, while Australia claimed a giant section.

Even the United States had an interest in the area. In 1939, the country launched the United States Antarctic Service Expedition, which enlisted more than one hundred people. The commander was Richard Byrd, an accomplished naval officer. By order of President Franklin D. Roosevelt, the expedition was to establish bases and collect scientific data. The project was abandoned in February 1941, however, due to conflict arising from World War II. But American concern with Antarctica's potential would continue, resulting in the establishment of a base whose primary purpose was to support

Richard Byrd using a sextant, a tool to determine altitude. Byrd explored Antarctica by plane.

scientific research. Other countries, however, accused the United States of secretly trying to establish greater political influence over the area.

The Antarctic Treaty

By the 1950s, it became clear among leading nations that some kind of agreement had to be forged over the shared sovereignty of the Antarctic continent. The true beginning of this agreement came with the International Geophysical Year (often

A vehicle called a Tucker Sno-Cat balances on the edge of a crevasse during the Commonwealth Trans-Antarctic Expedition of 1957. To this day, Sno-Cats are much loved by many people in Antarctica, and a few are still used there.

referred to by its acronym, IGY), which occurred from 1957 to 1958. In basic terms, the IGY was an attempt by scientists from numerous countries to collect scientific information across the globe and share it. More than sixty-five nations took part. Research areas included space exploration, oceanography, geology, seismology, cartography, and more. One of the regions scientists wanted to examine in greater depth was Antarctica. This may not have occurred, however, if governments hadn't first agreed on who controlled what region.

International interest in Antarctica led to the Antarctic Treaty. The treaty formally established the area known as Antarctica, at least for political purposes, as all landmasses and ice masses that exist south of 60°S. It also erased any past claims of sovereignty on the continent, meaning that no one nation had absolute authority over any part of it. This would prevent any future conflicts between nations concerning influence in the region. The treaty also made it clear that

Herman Phleger, an American diplomat who served as the chairperson of the Antarctica Conference, signs the Antarctic Treaty on behalf of the United States in 1959.

Antarctica was to be used only for peaceful purposes, specifically for science. Thus, any type of commercial or military activity would not be permitted.

The treaty was negotiated in Washington D.C., and signed in 1959, and after further debate and revision, went into effect in 1961. At the time, twelve nations had signed it: the United States, the United Kingdom, New Zealand, Australia, Argentina, Chile, and a handful of others, all of whom had already established bases on the continent.

More Recent Developments

Many developments concerning the Antarctic Treaty have taken place in the years since it went into effect.

The Antarctic Treaty

The Antarctic Treaty consists of fourteen articles:

- Article I: There shall be no aggressive military activity in the Antarctic, although military personnel and equipment are permitted for peaceful purposes.
- Article II: Scientific research may be conducted freely.
- Article III: All scientific data used and collected will be offered openly to other nations in the interest of scientific research.
- Article IV: The treaty does not recognize past territorial claims of sovereignty in the region.
- Article V: Nuclear testing and the disposal of nuclear waste are prohibited.
- Article VI: The terms of the treaty apply to all land and ice south of 60°S, but not to the bodies of water.

Unloading supplies

- Article VII: All supplies sent to the Antarctic shall be open to inspection at any time, by any nation participating in the treaty.
- Article VIII: Scientists and others are bound by the laws of their own nation, even if they are working with those of other nations.
- Article IX: Nations participating in the treaty shall meet regularly.
- Article X: All nations participating in the treaty will work to ensure that no activities take place that are against the aims of the treaty.
- Article XI: Any disputes between participating nations concerning the treaty will be settled among themselves or by the International Court of Justice.
- Article XII: The terms of the treaty can be modified at any time, but only through unanimous agreement of participating nations.
- Article XIII: Any nation wishing to participate in the treaty must fully agree to its terms.
- Article XIV: The treaty becomes legally binding on June 23, 1961.

Abandoned oil drums

Additions have been made to the treaty, and scientific research has progressed at remarkable speed. About two hundred recommendations have been added to the treaty. They include efforts to conserve plant and animal life and the prohibition of mining.

Other nations have also gotten involved. The original twelve countries that signed the treaty all had an interest in the Antarctic region. Today, there are fifty-three participating nations. Each is classified in one of four categories:

1. Those with consulting power that continue to make a territorial claim in the region.
2. Those with consulting power that do not have a territorial claim in the region but leave open their right to make one in the future.

In 1988, people gathered at McMurdo Station to protest mining in Antarctica.

3. Those with consulting power that make no territorial claim in the region now or in the future.

4. Those that have no consulting power.

"Consulting power" means that the country can vote during meetings. Countries reach consulting status by proving they have an interest in the continent or conducting substantial scientific research there. Nonvoting nations are still welcome to attend the meetings. The majority of the nations participating in the treaty fall into the third category, with only a handful in the first. The United States is in the second category. Recent nations to join the treaty include Iceland,

South Africa has been sending researchers to Antarctica since 1962. The current base, SANAE IV, was built in 1997 and houses scientists and staff year-round.

An Indian scientist holds an ice core sample. India ratified the Antarctic Treaty in 1983.

Kazakhstan, and Mongolia. As concern about the Antarctic environment and understanding of the value of the scientific research performed there grows, it is likely that more nations will agree to participate in the treaty.

Government Today

A body called the Antarctic Treaty Secretariat is in charge of administering the Antarctic Treaty. The Antarctic Treaty Secretariat was formed in 2003 at the annual treaty meeting and formally began operations in September 2004. Its functions include maintaining records, overseeing the exchange of information between nations, managing meetings, and educating the public. The headquarters of the secretariat is in Buenos Aires, Argentina.

XXXIX REUNIÓN CONSULTIVA DEL TRATADO ANTÁRTICO

SANTIAGO - CHILE 2016

25 AÑOS DEL PROTOCOLO SOBRE PROTECCIÓN AMBIENTAL

Representatives of the nations involved with the Antarctic Treaty hold a meeting every year.

The Executive Secretary

The closest Antarctica really has to a political leader is the executive secretary of the Antarctic Treaty Secretariat. Today, that person is Manfred Reinke of Germany, who was appointed to the position by representatives of the consulting nations in 2009. Reinke is a marine biologist as well as director of the Alfred Wegener Institute for Polar and Marine Research in Bremerhaven, Germany. Reinke believes that the executive secretary's highest concern must be environmental preservation and protection of the region. To this end, the executive secretary goals include supporting ongoing research, increasing public awareness about Antarctica, and improving communication between treaty nations. He also believes it is critical to regulate the expanding field of Antarctic tourism.

CHAPTER 6

Science
and
Tourism

ANTARCTICA DOES NOT HAVE AN ECONOMY IN the traditional sense. There are no supermarkets, no shopping malls, no factories. But the continent does host activities that benefit the economies of various nations around the world.

Scientific Research

The great majority of work in Antarctica is related to scientific research. The continent is recognized by many governments around the world as a scientific preserve and is protected by international law against almost all other activities. About seventy-five permanent research stations are located in Antarctica. Most are along the coastline or on islands north of the continent. A few are farther inland in Antarctica, and one is right at the South Pole—the Amundsen-Scott South Pole Station. About thirty countries are represented by these stations. The total population of resident researchers reaches

Opposite: **A scientist adjusts a telescope at the South Pole. The South Pole is an excellent place to view space because it is very dry and at a high elevation. With little water vapor in the thin atmosphere, scientists have a clear view of distant objects.**

Scientists drill an ice core sample in Antarctica. They have found tiny microbes living in super salty water at subzero temperatures more than 100 feet (30 m) below the surface. These microbes are part of a group of life-forms known as extremophiles because they live in extreme conditions.

about four thousand in the summer season and then drops to only about a thousand for the winter. Thus, stations can be placed in one of two categories—year-round and seasonal. The seasonal stations usually sit dormant during the coldest months of the Antarctic winter.

Many research projects are being conducted in Antarctica at any given time. One group, for example, is currently studying the increasing concentration of carbon dioxide in the Southern Ocean, an effect of global warming and other environmental changes. Another group is studying the effects of the solar wind, a stream of particles released from the Sun, on Earth. These particles can affect Earth's magnetic field. Researchers in Antarctica study glaciers, geology, and the atmosphere. They peer into the distant reaches of the universe and look at ecosystems at the bottom of the sea. Antarctica has proven to be endlessly useful as the site for scientific research.

Like almost every nation in the world, Antarctica uses the metric system as its system of weights and measures. The only three countries that do not use the metric system are Liberia, Myanmar, and the United States. Antarctica uses the metric system because of the simple fact that the majority of countries represented by the treaty use it.

Tourism

For centuries, people have been curious about the land at the southern end of the globe, and Antarctica continues to attract hardy travelers today. An increasing number of people are willing to spend the time, money, and energy it takes to visit

Learning to Cope

Some scientists in Antarctica are there to study others who live there. Being in such an isolated environment, with periods of both continual light and dark, in extreme cold, in the company of the same people day after day, can be difficult. These extreme conditions sometimes can result in depression and other problems. Psychologists are working to understand what can be done to help people cope with working in Antarctica. What they learn could also help astronauts, people who work on deep-sea fishing boats, and others who work in extreme or isolated situations.

Science and Tourism   **77**

the frozen land. In 2000, about fifteen thousand people visited the continent. Today, about thirty-eight thousand people visit the continent every year.

The earliest examples of Antarctic tourism occurred when mail and supply ships visited the region in the 1920s to make deliveries at whaling stations. Sometimes these ships would bring along people who had paid just to visit. This early tourism occurred only occasionally for the next few decades. It wasn't until the mid-1960s that tourism in Antarctica began to increase. At the time, a Swedish businessperson named Lars-Eric Lindblad began offering tourist trips to Antarctica and other remote and unusual places around the globe. In the late 1970s, Australia and New Zealand began offering tourist flights over Antarctica. These flights did not land because there was no commercial airport on Antarctica, but travelers could see the land through the plane windows.

Today, Antarctica has some airstrips, but they are used almost exclusively by

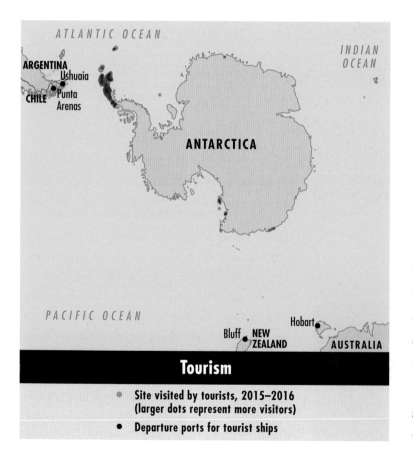

ATLANTIC OCEAN

INDIAN OCEAN

ARGENTINA
Ushuaia
CHILE Punta
Arenas

ANTARCTICA

PACIFIC OCEAN

Hobart
Bluff NEW
ZEALAND
AUSTRALIA

Tourism

• Site visited by tourists, 2015–2016 (larger dots represent more visitors)

• Departure ports for tourist ships

researchers. For tourists, the most common way to visit Antarctica is still by boat. Some cruise ships stop along the Antarctic coast as part of a longer journey. If the ship has more than five hundred passengers, no one is allowed to come ashore. If the ship has fewer than five hundred passengers, tourists are allowed to leave the ship, however only one hundred people can come ashore at a time. Those who get to go ashore most likely do so somewhere along the Antarctic Peninsula, where the weather is mildest. Popular sites include Port Lockroy, a site on Wiencke Island off the Antarctic Peninsula. Once a British research station, it is now a museum.

Tourists gather on the deck of a huge cruise ship as it approaches the Antarctic coast.

Antarctic Historic Sites

Several fascinating historical sites have been preserved in Antarctica. On Inexpressible Island, there's an ice cave that was dug by the British Antarctic Expedition in 1912, and a sign they made is still visible. You can even see some of the bones of the seals they ate. On Ross Island is a cross that was put up on Wind Vane Hill to honor three people who died during Ernest Shackleton's Imperial Trans-Antarctic Expedition.

One of the most popular sites in the Antarctic region is the South Georgia Museum. It is located in Grytviken in what was once the home of a whaling station's manager. The museum includes exhibits concerning past explorations and surveys, mountaineering, natural history, fishing, and Shackleton's successes and tragedies. The museum is open from October to March and is popular with tourists, hosting about seven thousand visitors each season.

Some visitors spend a longer time on the continent. They might hike, ski, climb, or even camp overnight. Such visits can be made only in the warmer months.

Despite the existence of the Antarctic Treaty, it remains unclear which rules of which nations bind visitors. As a result, the Antarctic travel industry largely governs itself. In any case, all visitors are bound by the laws of their home nation as well as those set out by the treaty.

Fishing

One of the few major commercial practices in the Antarctic region is fishing. Fishers have been working in the Southern Ocean since the early eighteenth century. Back then, no one thought about regulating fishing because the harvests were plentiful and seemingly endless. But over the centuries, the fishing boats were taking in ever larger hauls. As the reliability of seabound transportation advanced throughout the twentieth century, fishermen were able to move about more freely in the region to seek out the next great hoard. By the late 1960s

Problems with Tourism

Although visiting Antarctica is an exciting adventure for tourists, it is also a concern. The steady flow of people can affect the environment and harm the Antarctic ecosystems. In 1989, for example, a ship sank in a harbor on the Antarctic Peninsula, and thousands of gallons of fuel leaked into the surrounding waters and impacted the local wildlife. Another tourist ship sank in 2007, spilling more fuel.

People are also concerned about the safety of tourists in such an extreme environment. Tragedies happen. Boats sink and people get hurt in the frigid environment. The worst tourist tragedy in Antarctic history occurred in 1979, when Air New Zealand's flight 901 crashed. The jet was on a sightseeing tour, flying at a low altitude so passengers could get a good view of the landscape. There was an error in the flight plan, however, and the plane crashed into Mount Erebus, killing all 257 people on board.

and early 1970s, industrial fishing operations had severely depleted populations of fish and other marine life and altered the Southern Ocean environment. World governments had to take action.

The result was a treaty called the Convention on the Conservation of Antarctic Marine Living Resources (CAMLR Convention). It specifically addressed one of the most alarming problems, that of the widespread depletion of krill, tiny creatures that provide nutrition to thousands of other species.

A fisher in the Southern Ocean holds a Patagonian toothfish.

But krill are also valuable to the fishing industry, and by the 1960s were being harvested on a large scale. This threatened all the species that feed on the krill. The treaty, which was adopted in 1980, limited the areas where krill could be harvested. It now forms the basis for fishing regulations in and around the Antarctic region.

Overharvesting krill threatens the survival of many other species.

From the Antarctic to Your Table

Today, commercial fishing still takes place in the Antarctic region. Boats from many countries travel to the Ross Sea to fish for species such as mackerel icefish, Patagonian toothfish, and Antarctic toothfish. In the United States, toothfish are usually sold under the name Chilean sea bass. Because they grow slowly and are increasingly popular, toothfish numbers have been dropping to critical levels. Although limits have been placed on fishing for these species, many people believe more needs to be done.

Science and Tourism **83**

Today, whaling is an intensely regulated industry and operates on a much smaller scale than in years past. Environmental activism has played a significant role in the reduction of the industry, as has diminishing public demand for whale products. The International Whaling Commission keeps a tight rein on all remaining commercial activities worldwide and banned the practice altogether in the Southern Ocean in 1994. Still, some nations have been caught whaling in the Southern Ocean in recent years. Japan, for example, harvested numerous Antarctic minke whales under the guise of scientific

A Japanese ship lifts a whale out of the ocean. Each year, the Japanese kill hundreds of whales in the Antarctic.

research. Although the International Court of Justice ordered Japan to cease its Southern Ocean whaling program in 2014, the Japanese have continued hunting the Antarctic minke whales, and the controversy continues.

Japanese officials at the International Court of Justice

Money . . . Sort of

Antarctica has no permanent population, no formal government, and no place to spend money other than at research stations where one might buy toothpaste or a souvenir. So you might think it wouldn't have any need for its own currency. But there is Antarctic money . . . sort of. A series of banknotes has been designed and produced for the purpose of collecting by an outfit called the Antarctica Overseas Exchange Office. This company, which has been in business since the 1990s, offers bills that look like "real" money, with scenes of penguins, mountains, and explorers. These bills cannot actually be used as money in Antarctica or anywhere else, but they are popular collectors' items. A portion of the profits is used to support scientific programs.

CHAPTER 7

The People Who Live There

ANTARCTICA DOES NOT HAVE A PERMANENT
population. So from the standpoint of an official count of the
people, the population would be zero, because everyone who is
there is living there temporarily. But at any given time, there
are a few thousand people on the continent. Some stay for a
few weeks, while others might be there for a year or two.

Researchers

Most of the people in Antarctica are researchers seeking scientific knowledge. There are roughly four thousand residents
during the warmer months, about one thousand during the winter, and another one thousand conducting research on ships in
the Antarctic waters. Since the researchers come from different
parts of the globe, Antarctica is a cultural melting pot.

Opposite: **People from all
over the globe work in
Antarctica.**

The First Antarctican

On January 7, 1978, a boy named Emilio Palma was born at Esperanza Base to Argentine parents. He was the first child known to have been born on the Antarctic continent.

The scientific research station with the largest population is McMurdo Station. It belongs to the United States and is located at the southern end of Ross Island. McMurdo Station was established in the mid-1950s and today can house more

People working in Antarctica travel there on large military cargo planes.

A gardener tends to lettuce in a greenhouse in Antarctica. The vegetables are grown hydroponically—in water rather than in soil.

than a thousand people. McMurdo is more than simply a research station. It has several airfields, a heliport, a harbor, a post office, a hospital, a gymnasium, a barbershop, a church, a bar, phone and Internet service, a disc golf course, and an ATM. Most of the people who live at McMurdo are not scientists. Instead, they are support staff—mechanics, cooks, doctors, custodians, firefighters, and so on.

Two settlements, the Argentine Esperanza Base and Chile's Villa Las Estrellas, welcome researchers' families. For residents who have young children, schooling and day care are available. Esperanza and Villa Las Estrellas are the locations on the continent that come closest to being ordinary towns. Both are located on King George Island. Villa Las Estrellas is the larger of the two, with a population of about 150 in the warmer months and about half that in the winter. In addition to its school, it has a hospital, a government office, a hotel for visitors, a gymnasium, and a souvenir shop. There is tele-

The red houses of Esperanza spread out above Hope Bay on the Antarctic Peninsula.

The majority of people living in Antarctica at any given time are Americans. In the summer months, Americans number about 1,300, roughly a third of the total Antarctic population. During this time of year, several hundred Argentines and a few hundred Russians, Chileans, and British people are also living in Antarctica. Other nations that routinely have researchers working in the Antarctic include Australia, Japan, Italy, and France. Scientists in Antarctica can come from any nation.

phone, television, Internet, and radio service, and there's an airport nearby. From the sky, Las Estrellas looks like a group of well-spaced buildings of simple construction set in the middle of a snowy plain.

A welcome sign at Villa Las Estrellas on King George Island shows the settlement's population.

The People Who Live There **93**

Another notable attempt at colonization was made by Chile in late 1984. Hoping to make progress not just with scientific studies but also mining and tourist interests, the Chilean Air Force sent several families to live on King George Island, which lies just off the tip of the Antarctic Peninsula.

Workers put together a building at a station in Antarctica in 1961.

A Chilean settlement on King George Island

Although some nations participating in the treaty did not like this idea, the Chilean government pointed out that these people were pioneers who would make life there easier for future residents. Food and other critical supplies were provided to the colony by air on a monthly basis. A television station broadcasts news and children's programming from the Chilean mainland.

But there were also problems that were inevitable for people living in an isolated environment with little to do. Some people became bored or depressed, and others had trouble getting along with each other. Children became tired of the same games and same playmates. Chile had a plan to introduce another twenty families, build a gymnasium, a shopping center, and a visitors' lodge, and then begin earning income from tourism. From there it was hoped that word would spread about the community and other people would volunteer to

Brazilian children slide down a hill in Antarctica.

move down. Chilean leaders also believed mining interests would provide the basis for an economy strong enough to support a small town. None of this panned out.

Many research bases have small shops.

A Warmer Tomorrow?

As the global climate changes and Earth's temperature rises, the temperature in Antarctica is also rising. Some experts believe that the effects of global warming could make certain areas of Antarctica more suitable for human life. In the northern parts of the Antarctic Peninsula, for example, it is possible that the land might defrost enough and the temperature increase enough to allow crops to grow. Under such conditions, people could survive more comfortably on the Antarctic continent. If temperatures continue to increase at the same rate, these changes could occur in the next hundred years.

CHAPTER 8

Faith and Folktales

IN MOST PLACES AROUND THE GLOBE, MYTHS AND folklore developed over hundreds or thousands of years. But Antarctica does not have a long established population, so a local mythology never arose there. Some folklore from other parts of the world, however, concern Antarctica.

Mythology and Folklore

Most Americans have heard of Bigfoot, the tall and hairy creature that supposedly lives in the forests of the Pacific Northwest, and the Loch Ness Monster, a dinosaur-like creature that is said to inhabit Loch Ness, a lake in Scotland. But far fewer have heard of the *ningen*, a beast that is said to live in the frigid waters around Antarctica.

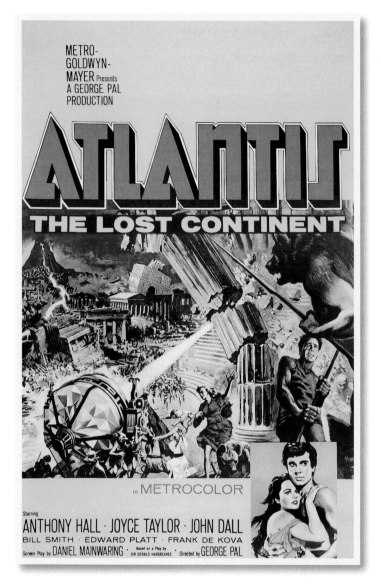

The lost continent of Atlantis has been the subject of many books and films.

The name comes from the Japanese word for *human*. It is fitting that the name is Japanese, because the legend seems to have originated with Japanese fishers. It is said that a ningen is about 75 feet (23 m) in length, with a smooth and pale torso; long, thin arms and legs; and a rounded head with simple eyes and a straight slit for a mouth. Some say the creature has a mermaid-like tail instead of legs. Ningens are said to live in seas all over the world, but they favor the icy waters of the Antarctic.

In the mid-2000s, public curiosity about ningens reached feverish heights in Japan. During that time, a magazine focusing on extraordinary events published an article with pictures that seemed to show some type of white masses floating through the waters of the Southern Ocean. This began a steady stream of reports from other people claiming to have seen ningens. Speculation over what those figures could actually be includes a large marine species that has yet to be identified (a large ray, for example), or simply hunks of ice that have the vague shape of a human. Whatever the case, ningens have stirred the imagination of many and are the closest thing Antarctica has to a local myth.

Another bit of folklore, one that has intrigued people for generations, is the lost continent of Atlantis. According to the story, Atlantis was a prosperous, powerful, technologically advanced society, populated with people of tremendous intellect and insight. Eventually, the continent was swallowed whole by the ocean. The story of Atlantis began in literature—the Greek philosopher Plato, for example, wrote about it while criticizing the arrogance of advanced societies. Still, some people believe the ancient references to Atlantis are based on a real place that was lost. Many people have put time and money into searching for the ruins of Atlantis.

Antarctica has been considered one of Atlantis's possible locations. Some claim that the ruins of Atlantis's once-great civilization now lie trapped beneath a deep layer of Antarctic ice. Experts, however, think the idea of an Atlantis-Antarctica connection—or the idea of Atlantis as a real place at all—is absurd.

Religion

The people who work in Antarctica come from all over the world, so they bring with them a wide variety of religious practices. The majority of the scientists and other personnel who live in Antarctica identify as Christian. Roman Catholicism is the most common religion, but people are Presbyterian, Methodist, Lutheran, and Episcopalian. There are quite a

Trinity Church is a Russian Orthodox Church on King George Island. It was built in Russia and then shipped to Antarctica.

few followers of the Russian Orthodox faith because of the large number of Russian researchers there. Many Antarctic churches also offer services for those of other faiths, including Buddhism, Baha'i, and Hinduism. A number of people in Antarctica also follow Judaism and Islam.

The first churches in Antarctica were built in the early twentieth century. The Norwegian Lutheran Church, for example, was built in 1913 on South Georgia Island, a British possession northeast of the Antarctic Peninsula. The church was popular among whalers and fishers who were working in the area and became known as the Whalers' Church. In 1922, British explorer Ernest Shackleton died nearby on his ship, and his funeral was held at the Whalers' Church. The church

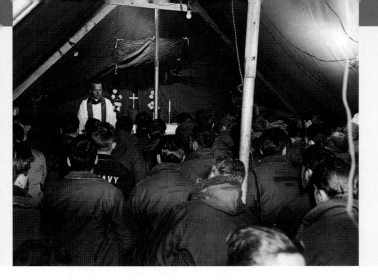

An Antarctic First

William Menster was the first member of the clergy to set foot on the continent of Antarctica. A U.S. Navy commander and Roman Catholic priest, he performed the first ever formal religious service on the continent in 1947. In a large tent, he led a service for two thousand people of a wide variety of faiths.

fell into disrepair shortly after World War II but has since been fixed up. Today, services are occasionally held there.

On the Antarctic continent, worship is held in many places. Some services are held in rooms that serve other purposes during most of the week. Others are fully dedicated

Services and weddings are occasionally held in the Whalers' Church on South Georgia Island.

A person plays guitar in the Chapel of the Snows.

churches with full-time ministers. There are at least seven churches on Antarctica. Although all the churches are Christian, people of other faiths are never turned away, and clergy provide services for people of every faith.

The Antarctic churches include the Chapel of the Snows, which is located on Ross Island as part of the McMurdo Station. It is a small white building that sits at the end of one of McMurdo's roadways. It serves both Catholics and Protestants and can comfortably seat about sixty people. Ministers do not stay on site for long periods but instead are rotated on a regular basis.

Another house of worship is Trinity Church, located on King George Island. It is Russian Orthodox and is located close to Russia's Bellingshausen Station. It is the southern-most freestanding church structure on earth. It was originally built in the Altai Mountains, in central Asia, and was taken apart and shipped to King George Island in the early 2000s. It has a weathered-gray appearance on the outside and a knotty-pine character on the inside. It has room for about two dozen visitors. As with other year-round churches on the continent, the clergy of Trinity rotate through, usually for a year. When ministers are not performing worship services, they tend to the spiritual needs of those at Bellingshausen Station. The first wedding ever held in Antarctica took place in Trinity Church in January 2007.

The Ice Cave Chapel

A particularly intriguing Antarctic church is the Ice Cave Catholic Chapel, located at Argentina's Belgrano II Base on the Weddell Sea. This church is in a cave carved out of solid ice. Since the temperatures never rise enough for the ice to melt, the structure is permanent. The church is essentially a series of inter-connected tunnels, one housing a small pulpit and a group of chairs. The church is easy to miss—it can be entered only through one iron door set at an angle into a small ice hill. Flags mark the entrance's location in case winds cover it with snow. The Ice Cave chapel has the distinction of being the southernmost house of worship of any design in the world.

Antarctica: A Year on Ice (2013), made by New Zealand director Anthony Powell, chronicles a year that Powell spent on Ross Island. He focused not just on himself but also on the people who live and work at the two research stations there—McMurdo (United States) and Scott (New Zealand). The film is an insightful exploration of their time at work and away from work, and the effects that living in Antarctica has on them both mentally and physically. The superb film

Anthony Powell sets up his camera in an ice cave during the year he spent in Antarctica.

earned Powell more than a dozen awards for best documentary. Another excellent documentary is *Shackleton's Antarctic Adventure* (2001), which tells the story of Ernest Shackleton's harrowing journey of 1914 to 1917.

The Written Word

The greatest literature to come out of Antarctica are the writings of the men who struggled and in some cases gave their lives to explore the continent. The writings of Robert Falcon Scott, Ernest Shackleton, and Roald Amundsen made vivid the excitement and horrors of their expeditions. One of the best accounts was *The Worst Journey in the World* by Apsley Cherry-Garrard, a member of Scott's 1910 to 1913 expedition. Cherry-Garrard's honest description of the journey that took Scott's life continues to mesmerize readers more than a hundred years later.

Many more recent books have been written about Antarctica, trying to capture the continent's natural mystery.

PENGUIN BOOKS

TRAVEL AND ADVENTURE

THE WORST JOURNEY IN THE WORLD

APSLEY CHERRY-GARRARD

TRAVEL AND ADVENTURE

COMPLETE   UNABRIDGED

The Worst Journey in the World was first published in 1922.

Adding Color

Argentine artist Andrea Juan, who was born in 1964, has been traveling to Antarctica since the mid-2000s to create art with the help of technology. One of her preferred methods of exhibiting Antarctica's beauty is to arrange colorful fabrics and temporary sculptures in beautiful landscapes and then photograph and film her creations. Her work has exposed thousands of people to the continent's elegance and has increased understanding that it needs to remain pristine for future generations.

whales, and Scott's ship. Ponting also brought a movie camera to Antarctica, becoming one of the first people to take short films there. Frank Hurley was part of Shackleton's 1914 to 1917 expedition and took extraordinary pictures of the ship trapped in ice and sinking.

Today, more and more artists are venturing to the continent for opportunities to capture its breathtaking beauty firsthand. Some go for the thrill of the experience. Others are on a mission to expose the public to Antarctica's many wonders and, hopefully, inspire the rest of the world to preserve it in the future. Several countries have programs that send artists to Antarctica. In the United States, for example, the National Science Foundation runs the Antarctic Artists and Writers Program, which supports artists, filmmakers, musicians, poets, and others in creating work in Antarctica.

Sports

Many people who work in Antarctica love playing sports. It's also good for them, as studies have shown that competitive physical activity helps fight off the ill effects of prolonged isolation. People based at McMurdo Station have access to a gym

A man works out at the gym at Palmer Station.

Running on Ice

All around the world are runners who like to push themselves to the limit. Some take part in marathons, running 26 miles (42 km). But even that is not enough of a challenge for some. How can it be made harder? Do it in Antarctica.

In 2005, Irish athlete Richard Donovan established the Antarctic Ice Marathon. For those who want a shorter race, there is the associated Frozen Continent Half Marathon.

Similar to Donovan's race is the Antarctica Marathon, established in January 1995. It is held each year on King George Island. It is the same distance as the Antarctic Ice Marathon, beginning at Russia's Bellingshausen Station and following a gravel path around the island past several other bases before returning to Bellingshausen. This race has become so popular that there are now tourist packages—requiring reservations years in advance—to bring in participants from all points around the globe.

that has a full-size basketball court, a fully equipped workout room, a climbing wall, and facilities for dodgeball and fencing. Many of the other stations on the continent have similar gyms.

Outside, a game of volleyball, baseball, or softball can occur anytime there's enough daylight. American football is generally avoided, since tackling people to the hard, icy ground just plain hurts. However, people from many countries engage in lively games of rugby, a sport where players can kick, pass, or run with the ball. Sports played in Antarctica are different than they would be on grass. Balls move a lot more on

icy surfaces than they do on grass or dirt. A well-hit grounder in baseball, for example, might skitter for a hundred yards or more if no one gets a hand on it.

People at the Amundsen-Scott South Pole Station toss around a football.

The Ross Island Cup

Research stations sometimes have friendly sporting competitions. One of the longest-standing is a rugby game between a U.S. team from McMurdo Station and a New Zealand team from Scott Base. The winner takes home the Ross Island Cup.

Rugby is one of the most popular sports in New Zealand, but it is not common in the United States. It is so rare there, in fact, that many of the Americans playing in the Ross Island Cup game have never played before. The New Zealanders have won the Ross Island Cup every time.

CHAPTER 10

Living on the Ice

LIVING IN ANTARCTICA IS DIFFERENT FROM LIVING just about anywhere else in the world. Long periods of sunlight are followed by long periods of darkness. Cold days are followed by colder days, and even colder. There are no shopping malls, no sports stadiums, no movie theaters. So what is life like for people who "live on the ice"?

Safety First

In Antarctica, one of the greatest priorities is safety, for everyone's sake. Although it is important to be mindful of safety no matter where you live, the extreme conditions in Antarctica make it all the more critical. As soon as people arrive, they are commonly given a crash course in safety basics.

Opposite: **Face masks are essential during many of Antarctica's cold days.**

Protecting the Skin

Skin damage is a constant danger in Antarctica—and it can happen fast. Sunburn is a major concern. During warmer times of the year, the sun not only shines intensely but also reflects off the snow. All that light combined with the naturally dry air and the winds can cause significant damage to exposed skin. Another type of skin damage, frostbite, can occur quickly if a person gets wet while being exposed to the elements.

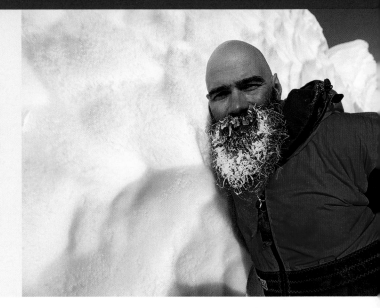

Frostbite—which can occur when parts of the body freeze—is a routine threat that has left people without fingers and toes. The weather can change suddenly. One minute it is calm and clear, and the next it is windy enough to blow a person over. Crevasses—breaks in the ice—are a particularly deadly danger, as people often don't notice them because they're covered by snow. Similarly, people can fall through sea ice. Also, people can easily become lost in whiteout conditions. These occur when the wind blows the snow into a thick fog. It is often so thick that people cannot even see the ground at their feet.

Commonsense safety measures include making sure generators are always in good working order; drinking plenty of water; always having warm, dry clothes on hand; keeping an emergency kit handy; and always watching the weather.

Mealtime

Cooking in Antarctica can be tricky. Supplies don't come in very often, so the chefs have to plan well. Every research station has at least one chef who is in charge of planning and preparing meals. The chef has to be very creative so as not to serve the same meals over and over again causing people to become bored. Cans of tomatoes, for example, can be turned into a variety of soups, pizzas, and chili. It is important to mix it up.

A chef makes pizza for people living at Great Britain's Halley VI Station.

Many fresh fruits and vegetables are only available when supply ships first come in. These foods are prized by everyone. A good salad loaded with crisp vegetables or a bowlful of berries is a treat. The fresh produce lasts only a few days, however, and it may be months before another supply arrives. The chefs then need to be extra creative, coming up with nutritious and delicious foods using dried and canned goods and ingredients such as carrots and tomatoes, which last longer than many vegetables.

The cafeteria at McMurdo Station offers many options.

A Seafood Lover's Paradise

Common dishes in Antarctica include pretty much anything that comes from the sea. Since the majority of research stations are located along the coast, a variety of seafoods can be obtained readily and then prepared fresh. Common fish found there include tuna, salmon, swordfish, halibut, and snapper. Also very popular are shellfish such as crabs, mussels, and clams. Soups made from shellfish are especially welcome, because they provide inner warmth. Sushi, which is made from raw fish, is not offered often, because it takes a great deal of effort to prepare in large quantities. Most people in Antarctica prefer their fish baked, broiled, or fried.

Chefs go out of their way to offer bright and colorful items whenever possible because people get tired of eating nothing but the browns and whites of pasta, potatoes, and rice day after day. In the white landscape of Antarctica, the pop of color from an apple, a strawberry, or an avocado is an important part of enjoying food. Meals are usually offered buffet style, with diners serving themselves.

For the most part, the people who live in Antarctica eat the same foods as people do elsewhere. But some minor adjustments have to be made because of the extreme conditions. For example, people who are out in the extreme cold need more protein and foods high in carbohydrates, such as pasta, chips, and cookies. Once they are out in the field and their bodies start burning energy reserves to maintain warmth, those calories will disappear fast.

Private Space

Everyone gets some—but not much—private space in Antarctica. There are no mansions or deluxe bedroom suites with fireplaces. Most research bases have dorm buildings where residents live. The rooms are simple, with cots or bunk beds. Two people often share a room, although in winter, when many people leave the continent, those who remain may get a

Scientists on an expedition across Antarctica sleep in simple bunks.

Antarctic Roadways

Some roads do cross the Antarctic landscape. They are not paved—some are dirt roads and others are ice roads, which often have to be cleared of snow that has blown onto them. Fortunately, these roads have been marked with flags so the route is always visible. One of the longest roads in the region is the McMurdo–South Pole Highway, or South Pole Traverse, which is nearly 1,000 miles (1,600 km) long and runs from McMurdo Station in the south, over the Ross Ice Shelf, through the Transantarctic Mountains, and finally to the Amundsen-Scott South Pole Station. Construction began in 2002 and took four years to complete.

room to themselves. There are several rooms per floor, and on each floor is a shared bathroom and shower. Some dorm buildings also offer a lounge room, which usually has comfortable chairs, couches, a television set, and a few other amenities.

Getting Around

There was a time when the fastest way to trek the Antarctic landscape was with a team of dogs tied to a sled. In 1994, the last dogs left Antarctica, however, for fear that they might spread disease to the native seal population. So how do people get around now?

Cars are rare on the continent. Even with snow tires, cars have a hard time traveling over the ice. Some Volkswagen Beetles are used, however, on the Australian bases. Some off-road vehicles with modified tires are also used. Their tires are wider than usual, have deeper treads, and are often kept at low pressure since tires that are fully inflated have a greater chance of losing traction. Snowmobiles are practical in certain areas.

The easiest way to travel long distances, although costly and with its own dangers, is through the air, either by plane or helicopter. Many bases have runways and helipads. These require a lot of effort to maintain because of the snow and ice. Weather conditions severely limit flying opportunities. In the winter, when there is around-the-clock darkness, flights are made only during emergencies. In that situation, the landing area may be marked on the ground by fires in barrels.

A snowmobile carefully crosses a fuel pipe marked by many flags.

Having Fun

When people living in Antarctica aren't working, they find ways to relax and enjoy themselves. In their rooms, people read, play on their laptops (Internet service is available at most Antarctic research stations), talk to friends and family back home, listen to music, play guitars or other instruments, and catch up on lost sleep. Those willing to venture beyond their dorm rooms, however, find quite a bit to do.

Pool is a popular pastime in Antarctica.

Many bases have the Antarctica version of a bar or café. Some have video games and pool tables. A group relaxing at a table might break out a board game or deck of cards. Parties are popular, often with costume themes because it's always fun to see if someone can put together a pirate outfit or look like a cartoon character using only the scant materials available. Outdoor activities such as hiking and skiing can be fun. Sometimes people go on long runs through the bleak but beautiful landscape that, for a few weeks or a few months, they call home.

Fast Facts

Official name: Antarctica

Official language: None. The most common languages are English, Spanish, Russian, Japanese, French, and Italian.

Drifting ice

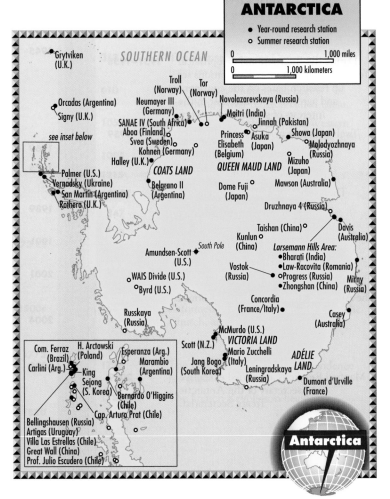

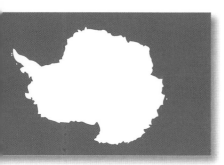

Antarctica flag

Sun over Antarctica

Official religion: None.

Type of government: Antarctica is collectively overseen by the participating nations in the Antarctic Treaty System.

Administrative head: Executive secretary of the Antarctic Treaty Secretariat

Area: 5,400,000 square miles (14,000,000 sq km)

Highest elevation: Mount Vinson, 16,050 feet (4,892 m) above sea level

Lowest elevation: Bentley Subglacial Trench, 8,383 feet (2,555 m) below sea level

Southernmost point: South Pole, 90°S latitude and 0° longitude

Northernmost point: Prime Head, at the northern tip of the Antarctic Peninsula

Average high temperature: At McMurdo Station, 32°F (0°C) in January, –7°F (–22°C) in July; at the South Pole, –15°F (–26°C) in January, –69°F (–56°C) in July

Average low temperature: At McMurdo Station, 22°F (–5.5°C) in January, –22°F (–30°C) in July; at the South Pole, –21°F (–29°C) in January, –81°F (–63°C) in July

Coldest recorded temperature: –136°F (–93°C) in August 2010

Warmest recorded temperature: 63.5°F (17.5°C) on March 24, 2015, at Hope Bay, on the Trinity Peninsula

Average annual precipitation: 6.5 inches (17 cm)

Fumerole on Mt. Erebus

Souvenir currency

Population: About 4,000 in the warmer months, and 1,000 in the colder months

Largest summer population by country (2016):

United States	1,293
Argentina	667
Russia	429
Chile	359
United Kingdom	217

Landmarks:
- ▶ *Ceremonial South Pole,* Amundsen-Scott South Pole Station
- ▶ *Emperor penguin migration site*
- ▶ *Ice Cave Chapel*, Belgrano II Base
- ▶ *Port Lockroy*, Wiencke Island

Economy: Scientific research is the only approved activity on the Antarctic continent. Commercial fishing, however, is common in the Southern Ocean. In addition, about 38,000 tourists travel to Antarctica each year.

System of weights and measures: Metric system

Researchers

Robert Falcon Scott

Prominent people:

Roald Amundsen (1872–1928)
*Norwegian explorer who was the first
person to reach the South Pole*

Frank Hurley (1885–1962)
*Australian photographer who documented
Ernest Shackleton's second expedition*

Andrea Juan (1964–)
Argentine artist who focuses on Antarctica

Manfred Reinke (?–)
*German marine biologist and executive
secretary of the Antarctic Treaty Secretariat*

James Clark Ross (1800–1862)
*British explorer who discovered the
Ross Sea*

Robert Falcon Scott (1868–1912)
*British explorer who led two
expeditions to Antarctica*

Ernest Shackleton (1874–1922)
*Irish explorer who took three British
research expeditions to Antarctica*

To Find Out More

Books

▶ Buckley, James Jr., and Max Hergenrother. *Who Was Ernest Shackleton?* New York: Grosset & Dunlap: 2013.

▶ Evagelelis, Irene, and David McAleese. *Antarctica*. San Diego: Classroom Complete Press, 2015.

▶ Ganeri, Anita. *A Year in Antarctica*. New York: DK Children, 2015.

Video

▶ *Antarctica: A Year on Ice*. Chicago: Music Box Films, 2015.

▶ *Frozen Planet*. London: BBC Home Entertainment, 2012.

▶ *March of the Penguins*. Burbank, CA: Warner Home Video, 2006.

▶ *Shackleton's Antarctic Adventure*. Chatsworth, CA: Image Entertainment, 2002.

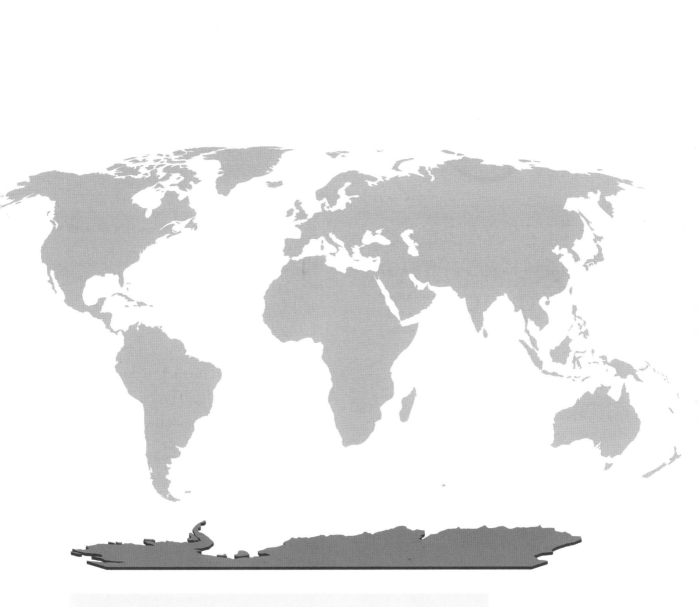

▶ Visit this Scholastic Web site for more information on Antarctica:
www.factsfornow.scholastic.com
Enter the keyword **Antarctica**

Index

Page numbers in *italics* indicate illustrations.

Meet the Author

WIL MARA IS AN AWARD-WINNING author of more than 185 books, many of them educational titles for children. He began writing in the late 1980s with several nonfiction titles about herpetology. He branched out into fiction in the mid-1990s, when he wrote five of the popular Boxcar Children Mysteries. He has since authored more than a dozen novels, including *Wave*, which was the recipient of the 2005 New Jersey Notable Book Award, *The Gemini Virus*, and the *New York Times* best seller *Frame 232*, which reached the #1 spot in its category on Amazon.com and won the 2013 Lime Award for Excellence in Fiction.

Photo Credits

Photographs ©: cover: Per-Andre Hoffman/LOOK-foto/Getty Images; back cover: Nigel Pavitt/AWL Images; 2: Ralf Hettler/iStockphoto; 5: Patrick Endres/age fotostock; 6 left: Deven Stross, NSF/United States Antarctic Program (USAP); 6 center: GentooMultimediaLimited/iStockphoto; 6 right: Ralph Lee Hopkins/Getty Images; 7 left: Jo Deleker/age fotostock; 7 right: Borge Ousland/National Geographic Creative; 8: Cliff Leight/Getty Images; 11: Getty ImagesPaul Nicklen/; 12: Robyn Waserman, NSF/United States Antarctic Program (USAP); 13: David Tipling/FLPA/age fotostock; 14: Norbert Wu/Minden Pictures; 16: Cliff Leight/Getty Images; 17: Deven Stross, NSF/United States Antarctic Program (USAP); 18: Bluegreen Pictures/Alamy Images; 19: Gordon Wiltsie/National Geographic Creative; 20: Colin Monteath/Minden Pictures; 21: Galen Rowell/Mountain Light/Alamy Images; 23: Buzz Pictures/Alamy Images; 24: Ralph Lee Hopkins/National Geographic Creative; 25: Michael Nolan/robertharding/Getty Images; 26: Cultura RM Exclusive/Brett Phibbs/Getty Images; 27: World History Archive/Alamy Images; 28: Yva Momatiuk and John Eastcott/Minden Pictures; 30: Sue Flood/Getty Images; 31: David Tipling/Getty Images; 32: David Tipling/FLPA/age fotostock; 33: GentooMultimediaLimited/iStockphoto; 34: Seapics.com; 35: Ralph Lee Hopkins/Getty Images; 36: Dan Guravich/Getty Images; 37: Jo Deleker/age fotostock; 38: Frans Lanting Studio/Alamy Images; 39: Ralph Lee Hopkins/Getty Images; 40: Doug Allan/Minden Pictures; 41: Tim Laman/National Geographic Creative; 42: North Wind Picture Archives, 44 top: DEA/G. Dagli Orti/Getty Images; 44 bottom: Fine Art Photographic/Corbis/Getty Images; 46: DEA/G. Dagli Orti/Getty Images; 47: Robert W. Nicholson/National Geographic/Getty Images; 49: VichoT/iStockphoto; 50: Robin Smith/Getty Images; 51: neftali/Shutterstock, Inc.; 52: Hulton Archive/Getty Images; 53: Chronicle/Alamy Images; 54: Herbert George/Library of Congress; 55: Philip and Elizabeth De Bay/Stapleton Collection/Corbis/Getty Images; 56: UniversalImagesGroup/Getty Images; 57: Library of Congress; 59: Frank Hurley/Scott Polar Research Institute, University of Cambridge/Getty Images; 60: Dwight Bohnet, NSF/United States Antarctic Program (USAP); 62: De Agostini Picture Library/age fotostock; 64: Eliot Elisofon/Getty Images; 65: Imagno/Getty Images; 66: Fox Photos/Getty Images; 67: rep0rter/iStockphoto; 68: Herman Phleger/Wikimedia; 69 bottom: Robert Hernandez/Getty Images; 69 top: Bai Yang/Xinhau News Agency/Newscom; 70: Greenpeace; 71: Dr. Ross Hofmeyr (c) 2008/SANAP/Wikimedia; 72: Pallava Bagla/Getty Images; 73 top: Mario Ruiz/EPA/Newscom; 73 bottom: Mario Ruiz/EPA/Newscom; 74: D.A. Harper-Cara/KRT/Newscom; 76: Jason Edwards/Getty Images; 77 top: Bettmann/Getty Images; 77 bottom: Maria Stenzel/National Geographic Creative; 79: ad_foto/iStockphoto; 80: Neil McAllister/Alamy Images; 81: Mitsuaki Iwago/Minden Pictures/Getty Images; 82: Paul Sutherland/Getty Images; 83 top: Flip Nicklin/Minden Pictures/Getty Images; 83 bottom: Ron Purdy/age fotostock; 84: Kean Collection/Getty Images; 85: Gircke/ullstein bild/Getty Images; 86: Greenpeace; 87 top: Martijn Beekman/AFP/Getty Images; 87 bottom: http://banknoteindex.com; 88: AFP/Getty Images; 90 top: Horacio Villalobos/Corbis/Getty Images; 90 bottom: Neil Lucas/NPL/Minden Pictures; 91: Ty Milford/Getty Images; 92: Steve Estvanik/Dreamstime; 93 top: TASS/Getty Images; 93 bottom: Ben Cooper/Getty Images; 94: Michael S. Nolan/age fotostock; 95: Kim Westerskov/Getty Images; 96: Albert Moldvay/National Geographic/Getty Images; 97: Vanderlei Almeida/Getty Images; 98: Marina Klink/LatinContent/Getty Images; 99 top: travelib/Alamy Images; 99 bottom: Zoonar/Christa Kurtz/age fotostock; 100: TASS/Getty Images; 102: Everett Collection; 104: Ben Cooper/Getty Images; 105 top: U.S. Navy, NSF/United States Antarctic Program (USAP); 105 bottom: Andrew Peacock/Getty Images; 106: Josh Landis, NSF/United States Antarctic Program (USAP); 107: Mike Sharp/Antarctic Logistics & Expeditions; 108: Jason Edwards/Getty Images; 110: Anthony Powell; 111: Colin Monteath/age fotostock; 112: George Roux/Wikimedia; 113: Herbert George Ponting/Library of Congress; 114: Andrea Juan – New Eden 5199 – SOOC photo – Antarctica 2012; 115: Kristan Hutchinson, NSF/United States Antarctic Program (USAP); 116: Joel Estay/AFP/Getty Images; 117 top: Peter Rejcek, NSF/United States Antarctic Program (USAP); 117 bottom: Steve Martaindale, NSF/United States Antarctic Program (USAP); 118: Borge Ousland/National Geographic Creative; 120: Gordon Wiltsie/Getty Images; 121: Medavia/ZUMA Press/Newscom; 122: Jason Edwards/Getty Images; 123: JudyDillon/iStockphoto; 124: Dan Dixon, NSF/United States Antarctic Program (USAP); 125: George Blaisdell, NSF/United States Antarctic Program (USAP); 126: Jason Edwards/Getty Images; 127: Jan Butchofsky/Alamy Images; 130 left: Norbert Wu/Minden Pictures; 131 bottom: Cliff Leight/Getty Images; 131 top: rep0rter/iStockphoto; 132 bottom: http://banknoteindex.com; 132 top: Galen Rowell/Mountain Light/Alamy Images; 133 top: Jason Edwards/Getty Images; 133 bottom: Herbert George/Library of Congress.

Maps by Mapping Specialists.